Mastering the New MacBook Air (the M4 Laptop)

A Comprehensive Guide for Everyday Users

Techruz Reads

Copyright

Disclaimer

This book is intended solely for educational purposes. The information provided in this guide is for informational and instructional use only and does not constitute professional advice. The views and opinions expressed in this book are those of the author and do not reflect the official policy or position of any company or organization.

This publication is not sponsored, endorsed, or affiliated with any commercial products, and no products are being promoted or sold through its content. Any references to specific products, services, or companies are provided solely as examples and for the sake of discussion. Readers are encouraged to conduct their own research and seek professional advice before making any decisions based on the information presented in this book.

By using this guide, you agree that the author and publisher are not liable for any errors or omissions, or for any outcomes related to its use.

Table of contents

Introduction

Welcome to *Mastering the New MacBook Air (the M4 Laptop)*, a guide written by Techruz Reads. Whether you're a student, a creative professional, or just someone who's accidentally discovered a passion for all things Apple, you're in the right place.

When I first picked up my smartphone, I thought I'd reached the pinnacle of personal computing—until I met the MacBook Air. Imagine the convenience of your phone, multiplied by a supercharged processor, a brilliant display, and a keyboard that actually makes typing feel like a joy rather than a chore. This guide is built on years of experience—not just with smartphones (where autocorrect occasionally leads to hilarious mishaps), but with computers that truly empower you to do more.

In these pages, you'll discover:

- **A hands-on walkthrough** of setting up your MacBook Air, as friendly as a tutorial from your favorite gadget guru.
- **Insider tips and tricks** that blend professional know-how with a pinch of humor—because learning tech shouldn't feel like a dry lecture.

- **Step-by-step navigation** through macOS, tailored for users of all levels, ensuring even the most hesitant new user can feel right at home.

So, buckle up (or just sit back, relax, and enjoy a cup of coffee) as we explore everything from the sleek design and powerful M4 chip to the seamless integration with your other Apple devices. With this book as your guide, you'll soon be navigating your MacBook Air like a seasoned pro, with a few chuckles along the way.

Chapter 1

Getting Started

This is the first step of your MacBook Air adventure! In this chapter, we'll walk you through unboxing your new MacBook Air, setting it up, and getting acquainted with everything that comes in the box. Think of it as the "first date" with your new device—exciting, a little nerve-wracking, but ultimately delightful.

Unboxing and First Impressions

When your MacBook Air arrives, take a moment to enjoy the experience. The packaging is sleek and minimalistic—much like the device itself. Here's what you can expect:

- **The Box:** Designed to protect your new tech gem, the box is both sturdy and stylish. It hints at the elegance inside.
- **The Unboxing Ritual:** Open the box with care (this isn't a T-rex egg—gentle does it). As you lift the lid, you'll see your MacBook Air snugly nestled in its compartment.

- **First Look:** Remove the laptop and take in its lightweight, slim design. Notice the refined finish and feel the quality materials—it's like meeting an old friend who's been groomed to perfection.

A little humor to keep things light: if you find yourself talking to your new MacBook Air like it's a prized pet, don't worry—many of us do! Just remember, it's ready to work as hard as you do.

Initial Setup and Activation

Now that you've had your unboxing moment, it's time to power up and start the setup. Follow these steps to get your MacBook Air up and running:

1. **Power On:** Open the lid, press the power button, and watch the screen come to life. This is the moment when your new companion truly begins its journey.
2. **Language and Region:** The setup wizard will prompt you to choose your language and region. Take your time here—it's like choosing your accent for a day of adventure.
3. **Connect to Wi-Fi:** Linking to your Wi-Fi network is crucial. Think of it as your MacBook Air joining the world's conversation. A strong connection ensures a smooth start.

4. **Apple ID and iCloud:** Log in with your Apple ID or create one if you don't already have it. This step links your device to the Apple ecosystem, ensuring all your apps, photos, and data are seamlessly synchronized.

5. **Personalization:** Customize settings like Siri, Touch ID, and other features to suit your needs. It's like setting up your workspace—you want everything just right for a productive day ahead.

Remember, the setup process is designed to be intuitive. Even if you're not a tech-savvy guru, the wizard will guide you through each step with clear instructions. And if you ever feel a bit lost, a quick online search (or a chuckle over a tech meme) is all it takes to find your way back.

Navigating the Packaging and Included Accessories

Once your MacBook Air is out of its box, you'll find a few essential accessories included:

- **Charger and Cable:** These are your lifelines for keeping your device charged during those marathon work sessions or binge-watching

weekends. Make sure to connect them to your
power source and your MacBook Air.

- **Documentation:** A small booklet or quick start
  guide will be tucked away in the packaging. It
  provides helpful hints and tips, much like a
  friendly neighbor sharing local shortcuts.
- **Additional Items:** Depending on the model,
  there might be extra items like a protective sleeve
  or adapter. While these aren't the star of the
  show, they play a crucial supporting role in your
  overall experience.

Treat this stage as a chance to organize your new tech
setup. Lay out the accessories, get familiar with where
everything is, and set up a dedicated spot where your
MacBook Air can shine—whether it's your study desk,
your kitchen table, or that cozy corner in your living
room.

By the end of this chapter, you should feel comfortable
with the initial steps of your MacBook Air journey. With
a bit of patience and a smile on your face, you're now
ready to dive into the world of macOS and discover all
the powerful features your device has to offer. Welcome
to the start of a smooth, productive, and yes, fun tech
experience!

Chapter 2

Understanding Your MacBook Air

Now that you've successfully unboxed and set up your MacBook Air, let's dive into what makes this sleek device tick. In this chapter, we'll explore the core features and design elements that set the MacBook Air apart, all while keeping things friendly, informative, and yes, a bit humorous.

A Closer Look at the M4 Chip and Hardware

At the heart of your MacBook Air is the impressive M4 chip. This isn't just a speed upgrade—it's a complete reimagining of what a laptop processor can do. Here's why it's a game-changer:

- **Performance Boost:** The M4 chip delivers lightning-fast performance, meaning that even your most demanding tasks, whether it's editing photos or juggling multiple apps, feel as smooth as butter.

- **Efficiency Meets Power:** You get a perfect blend of power and energy efficiency. It's like having a sports car that sips fuel rather than guzzling it.
- **Unified Memory:** With up to 32GB of unified memory, your MacBook Air can handle more tasks simultaneously without breaking a sweat. Even if you're a multitasking wizard, this device has your back.

Design and Display: Elegance in Every Detail

Apple is renowned for its design aesthetics, and the MacBook Air is no exception. Here's what to expect:

- **Slim and Stylish:** At just 11mm thick, your MacBook Air is as light as it is stunning. It slips into your backpack or tote bag with ease, making it the perfect travel companion.
- **New Color Options:** The addition of a fresh "Sky Blue" variant means your device can be as expressive as your personality—fun, vibrant, and undeniably stylish.
- **Liquid Retina Display:** The screen is a visual treat. With vivid colors, sharp details, and up to

500 nits of brightness, whether you're streaming a movie or working on a presentation, your eyes are in for a delight. And yes, it supports dual 6K external displays for those who like their workspace big and bold.

Camera, Audio, and Other Cool Features

While most of us have become pros at taking selfies with our phones, the MacBook Air has its own tricks up its sleeve:

- **12MP Front Camera with Center Stage:** Forget about awkward angles in video calls—the Center Stage feature ensures you're always in the spotlight. It's like having a personal cameraman who knows all your best sides.
- **High-Quality Audio:** Whether you're tuning into a webinar or enjoying your favorite playlist, the built-in speakers deliver crisp, clear sound that fills the room.
- **Seamless Integration:** The MacBook Air is designed to play nicely with your other Apple devices. From effortlessly sharing files to continuing your work from one device to another, everything just works.

Battery Life and Portability: Work Hard, Play Harder

One of the standout features of your MacBook Air is its long-lasting battery life. Here's how it keeps up with your busy lifestyle:

- **All-Day Battery:** With up to 18 hours of battery life, this laptop is built to keep pace with your day—from early morning meetings to late-night creative sessions.
- **Lightweight Champion:** Weighing in at just a few pounds, it's the perfect blend of performance and portability. Whether you're commuting, traveling, or just moving from room to room, your MacBook Air is always ready to go.

The Overall Experience: A Perfect Companion

Understanding your MacBook Air isn't just about specs and features—it's about the overall experience. Here's the takeaway:

- **User-Friendly Interface:** Apple has always prided itself on creating intuitive devices, and the MacBook Air is no different. Every feature is designed with you in mind, ensuring a seamless and enjoyable user experience.

- **Built for Every User:** Whether you're a student, a creative professional, or just someone who loves technology, the MacBook Air adapts to your needs. It's like having a tool that grows with you, offering everything from casual browsing to professional-grade performance.

By now, you should have a clearer picture of what makes your MacBook Air a standout device. It's not just a laptop—it's a carefully crafted blend of art and engineering, designed to make your everyday tasks simpler, more enjoyable, and maybe even a little fun. Get ready to explore macOS in the next chapter, where we'll guide you through navigating your new digital playground with ease and a smile.

Chapter 3

Navigating macOS

This is the heart of your MacBook Air—the macOS operating system. In this chapter, we'll explore how to navigate macOS with ease and a bit of humor, just like a friendly guide showing you the ropes at your favorite hangout spot.

Introduction to macOS

macOS is more than just a pretty interface—it's your gateway to productivity and creativity. Designed with user-friendliness in mind, macOS offers a smooth, intuitive experience that helps you focus on what truly matters: getting things done (and maybe sneaking in a laugh or two along the way). Whether you're a seasoned user or new to Apple's ecosystem, macOS is built to welcome you with open arms.

The Desktop, Dock, and Menu Bar: Your Digital Command Center

Imagine your desktop as your personal workspace, meticulously organized to keep you focused:

- **Desktop:** This is your primary canvas where files, folders, and shortcuts reside. Think of it as your digital bulletin board—tidy or creative, it's all up to you.
- **Dock:** The Dock is your quick-access bar for favorite apps and utilities. It's like a well-curated toolbox, always ready with the right app when you need it. Need a laugh? You might even have a quirky icon or two hiding in there!
- **Menu Bar:** Always positioned at the top of your screen, the Menu Bar is home to essential controls and system information. It's your go-to spot for checking the time, battery life, and even switching between apps with a click.

Navigating these elements is as simple as swiping your hand—almost as smooth as scrolling through your favorite social media feed.

Finder and File Management: Organize Like a Pro

Meet Finder, your friendly file explorer on macOS. Think of Finder as the digital equivalent of a super-organized closet:

- **File Navigation:** Quickly locate your documents, photos, and apps with intuitive search and categorization features.
- **Folder Management:** Create, rename, and rearrange folders as easily as moving items in a physical filing cabinet. It's so straightforward that even a sleep-deprived college student on exam day can find their notes without a hitch.
- **Spotlight Search:** Need to find that elusive file? Just hit Command ($\mathcal{H}$) + Space and let Spotlight work its magic. It's like having a personal assistant who knows exactly where everything is.

System Preferences and Settings: Customize Your Experience

macOS is all about making your experience uniquely yours. Dive into System Preferences to tailor your device to your lifestyle:

- **Personalization:** Adjust everything from your desktop background to screen saver, ensuring your MacBook Air feels like a true extension of yourself.
- **Accessibility Features:** Whether you need larger text, voice commands, or other enhancements, macOS has a suite of options to help everyone navigate with ease.
- **Security and Privacy:** Set up features like FileVault and Find My Mac to keep your data safe. It's a bit like having a digital security guard, keeping an eye on your important files.

Exploring System Preferences is as enjoyable as rearranging your favorite playlist—fun and rewarding!

Tips and Shortcuts: Work Smarter, Not Harder

Now that you're getting comfortable with macOS, here are a few insider tips to boost your productivity:

- **Keyboard Shortcuts:** Master shortcuts like Command (⌘) + C for copy, Command (⌘) + V for paste, and Command (⌘) + Tab to switch between apps. It's like having a secret language with your computer.

- **Mission Control:** Use Mission Control to view all your open windows and quickly switch between tasks. Imagine having a bird's-eye view of your entire digital workspace!
- **Gestures and Trackpad Magic:** Familiarize yourself with multi-touch gestures on the trackpad. Swiping between desktops or pinching to zoom feels almost like a magic trick you can perform every day.

These shortcuts are the little tricks that make your MacBook Air not just a tool, but a reliable partner in your daily adventures—be it work, study, or a bit of well-deserved play.

By now, you should feel much more at home with macOS. It's not just an operating system; it's a well-designed companion that's ready to adapt to your every need. As you continue to explore, remember that every click and swipe brings you one step closer to mastering your MacBook Air—one delightful discovery at a time.

Chapter 4

Built-In Applications and Tools

In this Chapter, we will explore the wonderful suite of built-in applications and tools that come with your MacBook Air. Much like discovering hidden gems on your smartphone, you'll find that macOS offers an impressive collection of apps that are designed to boost your productivity, spark your creativity, and keep your digital life well-organized—all wrapped in a sleek, intuitive interface.

World of Ready-to-Use Apps

macOS isn't just about great hardware—it's also about the software that makes your day easier. Whether you're browsing the web, managing emails, or diving into creative projects, your MacBook Air comes preloaded with a variety of applications designed with you in mind:

- **Safari:** Enjoy a fast and secure browsing experience with Apple's very own web browser.

With features like Reader Mode and robust privacy settings, Safari is as reliable as your morning cup of coffee.

- **Mail:** Manage all your email accounts in one place. Its clean interface and smart organization tools help you stay on top of your messages—no more digging through cluttered inboxes.
- **Calendar:** Schedule meetings, set reminders, and keep track of your daily agenda with ease. Think of it as your digital planner that never misses an appointment.
- **Notes and Reminders:** Jot down quick ideas or create detailed to-do lists. These apps are perfect for everything from grocery lists to brainstorming your next big project.
- **Messages and FaceTime:** Stay connected with friends, family, and colleagues through seamless text and video calling. With a few taps, you'll be chatting away like it's second nature.

Productivity and Creativity at Your Fingertips

Your MacBook Air is more than just a tool for everyday tasks—it's a powerhouse for creative and productive endeavors:

- **Pages, Numbers, and Keynote:** Apple's suite of productivity apps lets you create professional documents, spreadsheets, and presentations. Whether you're drafting a report or designing a slideshow, these apps are built to impress.
- **Photos, iMovie, and GarageBand:** For those who love to get creative, these apps transform your MacBook Air into a multimedia studio. Edit photos, craft compelling videos, or compose your next hit song—all without needing to download extra software.
- **Preview:** Don't underestimate this unassuming app. It's perfect for quickly viewing PDFs, annotating documents, and even performing simple image edits. It's like the Swiss Army knife of macOS applications.

Handy Tools for Everyday Navigation

Beyond the major apps, macOS is filled with useful tools that help you navigate and manage your digital workspace efficiently:

- **Spotlight Search:** Instantly find files, apps, and even definitions with just a few keystrokes. It's like having a mini assistant who knows exactly where everything is.

- **Siri:** Yes, even on your MacBook Air, you have Siri. Ask questions, set reminders, or simply have a bit of fun—Siri is there to lend a digital hand.
- **Launchpad:** Think of Launchpad as your app hub. With a quick gesture, you can view and open all your applications, making it easy to switch between tasks without missing a beat.

Tips and Tricks for Getting the Most Out of Your Apps

Here are a few insider tips to help you master these built-in tools:

- **Customize Your Dock:** Arrange your most-used apps in the Dock for quick access. It's like setting up your own personal toolkit right at the bottom of your screen.
- **Learn Keyboard Shortcuts:** Simple shortcuts like Command (⌘) + Tab to switch apps or Command (⌘) + Space to open Spotlight can save you time and make your workflow more fluid.
- **Utilize Continuity:** Seamlessly move between your MacBook Air and other Apple devices. Start an email on your iPhone and finish it on your Mac—technology that works as a team!

By now, you should feel more empowered to explore and use the built-in applications on your MacBook Air. Each tool is designed to be both powerful and approachable—perfect for users of all levels. So go ahead, dive in, and experiment. With a little practice, you'll be navigating your MacBook Air's software as smoothly as you scroll through your favorite social media app—with a dash of humor and a lot of confidence.

Chapter 5

Practical Use and Everyday Navigation

In this Chapter, we will shift gears from exploring macOS features to mastering the daily navigation and practical use of your MacBook Air. Think of this chapter as your friendly guide to turning all those amazing features into everyday productivity and creativity, with a touch of humor to keep things light.

Mastering File and Folder Management

One of the keys to a smooth digital life is staying organized. Here's how to tame the wild world of files and folders:

- **Organize Like a Pro:**
  Start by creating a logical folder structure for your documents, photos, and projects. Whether it's work files or personal memories, a little organization goes a long way—imagine your

digital closet where every file has its own neat shelf.

- **Using Finder Efficiently:**
  Finder is your trusty file explorer on macOS. Learn to:

  - **Create and Rename Folders:** Drag files into folders and label them clearly.
  - **Sort and Search:** Use the built-in sorting options and Spotlight (Command ⌘ + Space) to quickly locate any file.
    It's like having a digital librarian at your fingertips—minus the shushing!

- **Tags and Smart Folders:**
  Utilize tags to color-code and categorize your files, making it a breeze to filter through them later. Create Smart Folders that automatically organize files based on your criteria—think of it as having a self-updating filing cabinet.

Customizing Your Workspace

Your MacBook Air should feel as personal and productive as your favorite workspace. Here's how to make it truly yours:

- **Desktop Personalization:**
  Choose a background that inspires you—whether it's a serene landscape or a bold abstract art piece. Keep your desktop clutter-free by only placing essential shortcuts and folders.

- **Tailoring the Dock:**
  Arrange your most-used applications in the Dock for quick access. Remove any apps that you rarely use. The Dock is your quick-launch bar, so keep it neat and relevant to your daily needs.

- **Setting Up Mission Control:**
  Mission Control gives you a bird's-eye view of all open windows and desktops. Use it to switch between tasks effortlessly. It's like having a backstage pass to your digital performance.

Shortcuts and Efficiency Hacks

Speed up your workflow with a few smart tricks:

- **Keyboard Shortcuts:**
  Familiarize yourself with common shortcuts:

- ○ **Command (⌘) + C and Command (⌘) + V:** The classic copy and paste duo.
- ○ **Command (⌘) + Tab:** Switch between open applications swiftly.
- ○ **Command (⌘) + W:** Close active windows without the hassle.
- These shortcuts save time and make you feel like you're in on a little secret with your computer.

- **Trackpad Gestures:**
  Get comfortable with multi-touch gestures:

  - ○ **Swipe between pages:** Use a two-finger swipe to navigate back and forth.
  - ○ **Pinch to Zoom:** Perfect for getting a closer look at photos or documents.
- Mastering these gestures turns everyday actions into smooth, almost dance-like moves.

- **Spotlight and Siri:**
  Rely on Spotlight for quick searches and Siri for voice commands. They're like your digital sidekicks, ready to help you out when you're juggling multiple tasks.

Seamless Integration with the Apple Ecosystem

If you're already using other Apple devices, you're in for a treat:

- **Handoff and Continuity:**
  Start a task on your iPhone and finish it on your MacBook Air seamlessly. Handoff ensures that your workflow is uninterrupted, making transitions feel as natural as switching channels on your TV.

- **AirDrop:**
  Share files between your devices effortlessly with AirDrop. It's the digital equivalent of passing a note in class—quick, secure, and hassle-free.

- **iCloud Sync:**
  Keep your photos, documents, and settings in sync across all your devices. iCloud ensures that your important data is always at your fingertips, no matter which Apple device you're using.

By now, you should feel well-equipped to make your MacBook Air work for you every day. Whether you're managing files, customizing your workspace, or streamlining your workflow with handy shortcuts, these tips will help you navigate your device with confidence and ease. Remember, every great journey begins with a single click—and maybe a chuckle or two along the way. Happy navigating!

Chapter 6

Maintenance and Troubleshooting

We will delve into the art of keeping your MacBook Air in tip-top shape and tackling those occasional hiccups with confidence in this chapter. Think of this as your guide to ensuring your trusty laptop remains as reliable as your favorite pair of sneakers—comfortable, dependable, and ready for action.

Regular Maintenance: Keeping Your MacBook Air Healthy

Just like any well-loved gadget, your MacBook Air thrives on a bit of TLC. Here's how to keep it running smoothly:

- **Software Updates:**
  Regularly updating your macOS and applications ensures you have the latest features and security patches. Apple makes this easy with automatic updates, but it's good to check

manually now and then. Navigate to System Settings > General > Software Update to stay current.

- **Disk Utility:**
  Over time, your storage disk might develop minor issues. Using Disk Utility to verify and repair your disk helps maintain optimal performance. Find it under Applications > Utilities > Disk Utility.

- **Manage Startup Items:**
  Too many applications launching at startup can slow down your MacBook. Review and remove unnecessary login items by going to System Settings > General > Login Items.

- **Regular Restarts:**
  Restarting your MacBook Air periodically clears temporary files and refreshes system resources. Aim for a restart at least once a week to keep things running smoothly.

Cleaning and Physical Care: Show Some Love to Your MacBook Air

Your MacBook Air's sleek design deserves to shine. Here's how to keep it looking and feeling fresh:

- **Screen and Keyboard Cleaning:**
  Use a microfiber cloth lightly dampened with distilled water to gently wipe the screen and keyboard. This method effectively removes fingerprints and dust without harming the surfaces.

- **Avoid Eating and Drinking Nearby:**
  Crumbs and spills are the arch-nemeses of keyboards. Keeping food and beverages at a safe distance can prevent accidental damage.

- **Proper Storage:**
  When not in use, store your MacBook Air in a protective case to shield it from dust and potential scratches. Think of it as tucking your laptop into a cozy bed.

Battery Health: Energize Your MacBook Air

A healthy battery means a happy MacBook Air. Here's how to maintain battery longevity:

- **Optimal Charging Practices:**
  It's best to keep your battery charged between 20% and 80%. Occasionally allowing it to drain completely before recharging can help calibrate the battery.

- **Avoid Extreme Temperatures:**
  Batteries dislike extreme cold or heat. Using your MacBook Air in moderate temperatures ensures battery efficiency and longevity.

- **Check Battery Health:**
  Monitor your battery's condition by navigating to System Settings > Battery. If you see a "Service Recommended" message, it might be time to consult Apple Support.

Troubleshooting Common Issues: Quick Fixes for Everyday Glitches

Even the best of us have off days. Here's how to address some common MacBook Air issues:

- **Slow Performance:**
  If your MacBook Air is lagging, try closing unused applications and browser tabs. Utilizing

Activity Monitor (found in Applications > Utilities) can help identify resource-hogging processes.

- **Unresponsive Applications:**
  When an app freezes, force quitting can save the day. Press Command (⌘) + Option + Esc to bring up the Force Quit menu, select the troublesome app, and click "Force Quit."

- **Wi-Fi Connectivity Issues:**
  Restarting your router and MacBook Air can resolve many connectivity problems. If issues persist, consider forgetting the network and reconnecting.

- **Battery Not Charging:**
  Ensure your charger and ports are clean and free from debris. If the problem continues, resetting the System Management Controller (SMC) might help. Instructions for this can be found on Apple's support page.

By incorporating these maintenance and troubleshooting practices into your routine, your MacBook Air will remain a reliable companion for years to come. Remember, a little care goes a long way in ensuring your device performs at its best. And when in doubt, don't hesitate to reach out to Apple Support or visit an authorized service provider.

Chapter 7

Security and Privacy

Welcome to Chapter 7, where we delve into the vital aspects of securing your MacBook Air and safeguarding your personal information. Think of this chapter as your guide to transforming your Mac into a digital fortress—without the need for a moat or drawbridge.

Understanding macOS Security Features

Your MacBook Air comes equipped with robust security features designed to protect both your device and data. Let's explore these built-in guardians:

- **Gatekeeper:**
  This vigilant bouncer ensures that only trusted software runs on your Mac. When you download an app from outside the App Store, Gatekeeper verifies it's from an identified developer and free of known malicious content. It's like having a discerning doorman for your digital nightclub.

- **FileVault:**
  For those who like their data under lock and key, FileVault offers full-disk encryption. It encrypts your entire drive, ensuring that your information remains confidential, even if your Mac falls into the wrong hands.

- **Firewall:**
  macOS includes a built-in firewall that protects your Mac from unauthorized network access and potential denial-of-service attacks. It's your personal digital shield against unwanted intrusions.

7.2 Configuring Privacy & Security Settings

Taking control of your privacy settings empowers you to manage what information you share and with whom. Here's how to fine-tune these settings:

1. **Access Privacy & Security Settings:**

   - Click on the Apple menu and select **System Settings**.
   - In the sidebar, click **Privacy & Security**.

2. **Adjust App Permissions:**

   - Within the Privacy section, you'll find categories like **Location Services**, **Camera**, and **Microphone**.
   - Click on each category to view which apps have requested access.
   - Toggle permissions to grant or revoke access as you see fit. Remember, you're the gatekeeper of your own data.

3. **Set Advanced Options:**

   - Scroll down and click on **Advanced** to explore additional security settings, such as requiring an administrator password to access system-wide settings.

Best Practices for Enhancing Security

Beyond built-in features, adopting certain habits can further bolster your Mac's defenses:

- **Create a Standard User Account:**
  For daily activities, use a non-administrative account. This limits the potential impact of malicious software. Think of it as operating on a

"need-to-know" basis.

- **Disable Automatic Login:**
  Ensure that a password is required upon startup to prevent unauthorized access. It's like locking your front door, even when you're home.

- **Use a Password Manager:**
  Employing a reputable password manager helps you generate and store complex, unique passwords for all your accounts, reducing the risk of breaches.

- **Enable Two-Factor Authentication (2FA):**
  Add an extra layer of security to your Apple ID and other accounts by requiring a second form of verification. It's akin to a double-lock system for your digital life.

- **Regularly Update Software:**
  Keep your macOS and applications up to date to benefit from the latest security patches. It's the tech equivalent of eating your vegetables—essential for good health.

Protecting Against Malware and Phishing

Staying vigilant against malicious software and deceptive schemes is crucial:

- **Be Cautious with Downloads:**
  Only download software from trusted sources, such as the Mac App Store or reputable developers. If something seems too good to be true, it probably is.

- **Recognize Phishing Attempts:**
  Be skeptical of unsolicited emails or messages requesting personal information or directing you to unfamiliar websites. When in doubt, verify the source before clicking on any links.

- **Install Reputable Security Software:**
  Consider using additional security software to provide real-time protection against malware and other threats. Think of it as hiring a personal bodyguard for your Mac.

By familiarizing yourself with macOS's security features and adopting these best practices, you can significantly enhance the protection of your MacBook Air and personal data. Remember, in the digital realm, a proactive approach to security is your best defense. Stay safe, stay informed, and keep your digital drawbridge up.

Chapter 8

Accessibility Features

We will be talking about the myriad of accessibility features that make your MacBook Air not just a computer, but a device that adapts to a diverse range of needs. Whether you're navigating with your voice, eyes, or fingertips, macOS offers tools to ensure everyone has a seamless experience. Let's dive into this inclusive world, shall we?

Enabling Accessibility Features

Your MacBook Air is equipped with a suite of accessibility features designed to cater to various requirements. Activating them is straightforward:

1. **Open System Settings:**

    ○   Click on the Apple menu and select **System Settings**.
2. **Navigate to Accessibility:**

- In the sidebar, click **Accessibility**. Here, you'll find a categorized list of features tailored for Vision, Hearing, Mobility, and more.

3. **Explore and Activate:**

- Browse through the categories and toggle on the features that align with your needs. Remember, these tools are here to make your Mac experience as comfortable as possible.

Vision Assistance

For those who are visually impaired or simply prefer a different visual experience, macOS offers several tools:

- **VoiceOver:**

  - A built-in screen reader that provides spoken descriptions of what's on your screen. To activate:
    - Press **Command (⌘) + F5**.
    - Alternatively, if your Mac has Touch ID, quickly press it three times.
    - Or, ask Siri: "Turn VoiceOver on."

- **Zoom:**

  - Magnify the entire screen or a portion of it, making content easier to see.
- **Display Adjustments:**

  - Invert colors, increase contrast, or reduce motion to suit your visual preferences.

Hearing Support

macOS ensures that users with hearing impairments have a rich experience:

- **Captions:**

  - Enable real-time captioning for spoken audio from apps or live conversations. Customize the appearance to your liking.
- **Mono Audio:**

  - Combine stereo sound into a single track, ensuring you don't miss any audio content, especially if you have hearing loss in one ear.
- **Flashing Screen Alerts:**

- Instead of sound alerts, set your screen to flash when notifications arrive.

Physical and Motor Assistance

For those with mobility challenges, macOS offers features to enhance navigation:

- **Voice Control:**

  - Operate your Mac entirely with your voice, from opening apps to composing emails. It's like having a personal assistant who never takes a coffee break.
- **Keyboard and Mouse Alternatives:**

  - Features like Sticky Keys and Slow Keys make typing easier by modifying how keystrokes are registered.
- **Switch Control:**

  - Navigate your Mac using adaptive devices, allowing for customized control setups.

Cognitive and Learning Support

To aid users with cognitive or learning disabilities, macOS provides:

- **Reading Support:**

    - Utilize tools like Speak Screen to have text read aloud, aiding comprehension.
- **Simplified User Interface:**

    - Reduce visual clutter and distractions by adjusting display settings, helping focus on essential content.

By integrating these accessibility features into your MacBook Air, Apple ensures that technology is a bridge, not a barrier. Whether you need them temporarily or as a permanent aid, these tools are designed to make your computing experience as inclusive and user-friendly as possible. So go ahead, customize your Mac to fit your unique needs, and embrace the empowerment that comes with it.

Conclusion

As we draw the curtains on this comprehensive journey through the capabilities of your MacBook Air, it's evident that this device is more than just a tool—it's a gateway to a world of possibilities. From the foundational steps of setting up your Mac to the nuanced intricacies of customization, security, and accessibility, each chapter has been crafted to empower you with knowledge and confidence.

Your MacBook Air is designed not only for performance but also for personalization. By delving into its myriad features, you've unlocked the potential to tailor your computing experience to your unique preferences and needs. Whether it's enhancing productivity, safeguarding your data, or ensuring an inclusive user interface, the power lies at your fingertips.

Remember, the journey doesn't end here. Technology is ever-evolving, and so is your Mac. Stay curious, explore new features as they emerge, and continue to adapt your MacBook Air to serve you best. Embrace the learning curve, and let your Mac be a reflection of your individuality and aspirations.

In the words of Steve Jobs, "The people who are crazy enough to think they can change the world are the ones who do." Let your MacBook Air be the instrument through which you bring your unique contributions to the world.

www.ingramcontent.com/pod-product-compliance
Lightning Source LLC
Chambersburg PA
CBHW061054050326
40690CB00012B/2617